Mel,

Welcome to Saratoga!

Carol

(Overleaf, pages 2-3) Morning workout, Oklahoma Track
(Overleaf, pages 4-5) Turf racing, Saratoga Race Track
(Overleaf, pages 6-7) Greek Revival style home, Union Avenue
(Overleaf, pages 8-9) Table setting

Published by Thomasson-Grant, Inc., Frank L. Thomasson III and John F. Grant, Directors
Designed by Megan R. Youngquist
Text by Bernice Grohskopf and Elizabeth L.T. Brown
Edited by Carolyn M. Clark
Photographs copyright ©1986 by William Strode. All rights reserved.
Introduction copyright ©1986 by Heywood Hale Broun. All rights reserved.
This book, or any portions thereof, may not be reproduced in any form
without written permission of the publisher, Thomasson-Grant, Inc.
Photography may not be reproduced without permission of William Strode.
Introduction may not be reproduced without permission of Heywood Hale Broun.
Library of Congress catalog number 85-052217
ISBN 0-934738-19-X
Printed and bound in Japan by Dai Nippon Printing Co., Ltd.
Any inquiries should be directed to the publisher, Thomasson-Grant, Inc.,
505 Faulconer Drive, Suite 1C, Charlottesville, Virginia 22901,
telephone (804) 977-1780.

THOMASSON-GRANT

■ A SEASON OF ELEGANCE
SARATOGA

PHOTOGRAPHY BY WILLIAM STRODE
INTRODUCTION BY HEYWOOD HALE BROUN

If one had to pick a single word to epitomize Saratoga, it would be Romance. From its beginnings, the Spa has been a triumphant defiance of common sense and practicality, a place where hopes begin to seem like expectations, where fantasies look like investment opportunities.

Consider that the otherwise sensible Iroquois Indians were convinced that bubbling water from springs in a place they called Saraghtoque was a panacea for a spectrum of ailments. In proof of their belief, they carried Sir William Johnson, King George III's Indian agent, to the spring in 1761. They considered Sir William a friend and had named him "Man Who Does Much." Much of what he had done, however, had been in the direction of a good life which had left him in bad shape. We know that he rode to the springs in a litter and at least took a few steps on the way back, and we know that George Washington was so enthusiastic about Saratoga as a health resort that he tried to buy it.

We know, too, that over the years the place made the loftiest of aspirations look as practical as blueprints. So it was, at Saratoga in the 1930s that Helen Morgan, the immortal musical comedy star, the first and greatest "Julie" in "Show Boat," confided to racing writer Toney Betts over a dinner table that she longed to sing the title role in Jules Massenet's "Manon." Miss Morgan had a voice as beautifully shaped as a Japanese netsuke carving and just about as big, but over champagne and pressed duck she could hardly wait for the first notes of the overture. Everything seemed possible in a place where Romance draws dreams in indelible ink.

Pressed duck is a guess as to the dish which fed Miss Morgan's delusion, but it's certainly true that Saratoga is that rare American rural community where such comestibles are commonplace.

Early in the 19th century, a Saratoga sawmill operator named Gideon Putnam had the bright idea that people who had been drinking sulfurous waters just for their health might like to cover the flavor with something tasty for their pleasure. To this end he used the products of his mill to build a small inn beside one of the most noxious and successful upwellings and soon had to replace it with a larger hostelry. Today his name is attached to the state-run hotel which is agreed by all to be the inner holy for visitors during the August racing season.

Health and Hedonism—in the wedding of these opposites, symbolized by Putnam's first little hotel where cholesterol glazed the cure, is much of the romance of Saratoga. To have the best of both worlds, a long life and a merry one, is such an attractive idea that one no longer wonders why the aching, ailing Sir William Johnson let himself be jolted through the woods surrounding Saraghtoque.

Diamond Jim Brady, a steady visitor to Saratoga in the 1890s, spent many a morning bicycling with his friend Lillian Russell. From time to time the two hefties would stop and refresh themselves from a tank of orange juice, a regimen which would have done wonders for them if they had not sat down to pâté and pheasant for lunch.

Still, as someone with the improbable name of Sophie Sparkle wrote in "Sparkles from Saratoga" in 1873, "People who come here should be prepared to catch the inspiration of the hour; free from all care, lighthearted, willing and eager to enjoy life—to sip the foam when at its whitest—to catch the bubble while yet the rainbow glistens on it.

"A heart that is ready for all this is ready for Saratoga."

Such a heart is probably not ready for orange juice in the morning, but is probably ready for a day at the races, that bubble of excitement on which, for winners, the rainbow so colorfully glistens.

Ten years before Sophie Sparkle was rhapsodizing about snowy foam, a man named John "Old Smoke" Morrissey brought racing to the town. The four-day meeting was a modest forerunner to the modern month which is the only American answer to the pageantry of Royal Ascot.

Morrissey was not the sort of person with whom Sophie Sparkle would have cared to waltz. He was a bully politician, head of a New York City gang called the Dead Rabbits which, with clubs and fists, electioneered for Tammany Hall. It was his hope, in financing the race meeting, and six years later in building the luxurious gambling casino called the Saratoga Clubhouse, to earn social acceptance for himself and his wife Susie.

Sadly, Morrissey received nothing from the society patrons except checks for their losses, and the casino did not really flower until it fell into the hands of Richard Canfield, a Providence, Rhode Island gambler who had spent some time as a hotel clerk observing the behavior of the haute monde, and then six months in jail reading up on their wants and wishes.

What all this study produced was a place whose French chef, Monsieur Columbin, ran a legendary restaurant at a legendary loss—$70,000 in the first season—which drew gamblers of good taste from all over the country who ate with M. Columbin and went upstairs to gamble with Mr. Canfield in rooms where the top chip cost $100,000.

Aware that reformers regarded Saratoga as a sinkhole of sin which no healthful waters could wash clean, Canfield closed his club to women and on Sundays to everyone, but the racetrack was open to all six days a week, and from its beginnings was modeled on that English ideal of city elegance in country surroundings. Modern racegoers who have become accustomed to the glassed-in cubes which, like giant ant farms, enclose the all-weather fan as he watches the distant action, get the feeling at Saratoga that they have been transported by a time machine into a sporting print. Here the horses are saddled out under the trees and live in grass-rimmed barns where chickens, goats, and dogs in barnyard pro-

fusion walk among the thoroughbreds, who regard them as something between entertainers and mascots.

Here too, racing's dreams of glory begin. It is at Saratoga that the promising babies, the well-bred prospects for races with names and reputations, make their debuts. Here they will tell whether the owners who so hopefully handed out millions at the previous season's yearling sales have bought immortality or what will end up as half a ton of the most expensive pet food in the world.

Whatever their eventual records, they are all champions at the beginning of August in Saratoga. Where other tracks are content to fill their programs with short races for proven mediocrities, this old track comes as close as any to giving life to the cliché about racing as a means of "improving the breed."

For some, the racing world comes awake with the opening of the daily double windows, but for many in Saratoga, the best of times are the earliest of times—the hours just past dawn when the horses, snorting steam like so many handsome dragons, come out on the track for their morning workouts. One's concern at such times is untinged by thoughts of profit and loss. The chips have no value but the visions are beyond price. The outlines of the horses are beautifully sharp in the rosy light and the thudding of their hooves is not masked by the cheers of the bettors. They seem to run not to a goal or finish line but simply for the joy of the complex and rhythmic action which carries them so swiftly over the ground.

When Shakespeare's Henry V spoke of his favorite horse, he said, "When I bestride him, I soar, I am a hawk; he trots the air; the earth sings when he touches it."

It is doubtful that such elegant language runs through the minds of the exercise boys who guide the thoroughbreds on their morning gallops, but if you stand at the rail as they go by, you will, as often as not, hear them singing or whistling, perhaps in harmony with the earth beneath the hooves, and you will see smiles on their faces which, if less haughty than Henry's, are at least as joyous.

Then when you are full of the elevated thoughts which an overflowing measure of beauty brings, the sound of a bell will pull you back to the practical realities of a breakfast-free day. The bell heralds the arrival of the pastry and coffee truck which emerges from the trees along the backstretch to remind us that homely pleasures have also a place in the scheme of things.

Romance, said Joseph Conrad, "is that subtle thing that is mirage—that is life. It is the goodness of the years we have lived through, of the old time when we did this or that, when we dwelt here or there."

Saratoga, more than most places in evermore modern America, is full of visible evidence of the old time when the glow of romance seemed somehow brighter than the cool lights of today. Stark motel architecture and the frivolous impersonality of fast food signs dot the streets like blemishes in silk. But the total effect of the town is still such that one would not be surprised to see Berry Wall, the dandy who once won a bet in Saratoga by changing his clothes 40 times in a day, exchanging chat with Victor Herbert, the orchestra leader at the vast Grand Union Hotel who drove a beflowered pony carriage and wrote "Kiss Me Again" after hearing the phrase urgently whispered in the Grand Union's gardens. Proof of the opulence which created the proper setting for such characters as Wall and Herbert is found in the glorious excesses of the town's many "cottages." The exquisitely inappropriate designation of cottage is given to the summer palaces of society. It is the kind of wonderful understatement which makes Boston bankers refer to their lake and oceanside summer mansions as "camps" and is probably a product of Nanny's constant reminder that boasting about wealth should be left to those who had just acquired it.

A list of the cottages hangs on the wall of the racetrack's publicity office because most of the cottagers are owners of the newsmaking stables. Each year they hope to uncover a champion even as the elegant cottage furniture has its dustcovers removed in preparation for the round of parties at which successes will be toasted and failures treated with doses of champagne.

It would be an exaggeration to say that the cottages make Saratoga a rival to Versailles, but in a modest small town whose reason for being was for a long time the presence of gassy water rising through Potsdam sandstone, Laurentian gneiss, and blue clay, the presence of so many turreted, gabled, and cupolaed confections is a social historian's delight if occasionally a classical architect's nightmare.

Carrying on the tradition of understatement is the starkly named Saratoga Reading Room, which sounds like a dusty small-town library well stocked with the lesser novelists of the 1920s. It is, of course, nothing of the sort, being a beautifully appointed club where the reading is perhaps less important than the comfortable surroundings. It was in the Reading Room that Captain Harry Guggenheim, master of Cain Hoy Stables, had a private telephone installed so that he could deal with the commercial and social realities of the modern world without having to spend much time actually living in it.

That modern world, which Captain Guggenheim was keeping at a proper distance, for many years regarded Saratoga with some impatience as a place which took racing away from easily reachable Aqueduct and Belmont Park and carried it to what New Yorkers think of as a place midway between Albany and Tibet. When racing resumed after World War II, a complaint of popular editorialists was the loss of tax revenue which arose from shifting the sport to a place with a smaller volume of betting. Schoolchildren were depicted as doing without their state-supplied hot lunches while the rich munched caviar-mounded toast points and made their bets between sips of champagne.

It was the same kind of Spa-bashing which Nellie Bly, the round-the-world journalist, had done in 1894 when she referred to Saratoga as "Our Wickedest Summer Resort." She found the place "Money Mad by Day and Night" and in another headline was shocked to observe "Little Children Who Play the Horses," showing that one way or another Saratoga seemed to be bad for kids.

In recent years, however, a lot of people looking across the country's miles of malls and domino rows of condominiums, have come to the belated wisdom that Saratoga in its extravagant variety, its mixture of bucolic simplicity and gilded sophistication, is a phenomenon whose like is not going to be seen again. Unlike the false-fronted fantasy of reconstructed Americana—those places where actor-blacksmiths and actress-cookiemakers mimic ancestral trades—this place is real, functional, and fun.

In 1900 Saratoga had rooms for a tourist population of 20,000, a throng almost twice as big as the resident number on the census rolls; a ratio that has not been maintained as the town has about doubled in size.

Now that Miss Bly's strictures and those of later editorialists are forgotten, our wickedest summer resort has become one of our most beloved havens of nostalgia. The sins that Nellie Bly observed are now absent or irrelevant, and Saratoga, somewhat to the surprise of the racing community, has become, through such institutions as the Center for the Performing Arts and the Yaddo arts colony, one of the nation's cultural centers.

"Music in the morning inspires one to fresh activity," wrote Sophie Sparkle. "It incites to new energy; to noble impulses, and to lofty aims."

She was, of course, referring to concerts in which the dashing uniforms of the musicians were as inspiriting as the Victor Herbert melodies the band produced, jolly simple sounds as far away from the modern symphonic programs as the decorous waltzes of the 1890s are from the balletic patterns which modern dance companies bring to the big shed on the hillside.

It is even said that people come to the Spa who have no idea that over on Union Avenue there is one racetrack for thoroughbreds and not far away, another for harness horses; people who come only because they want to hear the sound of Brahms come drifting through the trees, a sound more complex than the single bell notes of the morning pastry wagon but as promising of satisfaction.

No one thinks of Saratoga as very wicked anymore except perhaps the rulers of Yaddo, that generous house of creativity where works are brought to fruition in an atmosphere of freedom and ease. Meals are provided, as are opportunities for walks on which the Muse may be met and asked for guidance, and there are opportunities for socializing and high-minded chat in amounts suitable to the temperaments of the artists.

There is only one firm rule. No one at Yaddo may go to the racetrack. The 400-acre former Trask estate has produced a string of successful artists, musicians, and writers, but if any of them has had the daily double, the fact has not been publicized.

As one who has yet to produce anything distinctive in the art line, this writer must confess that he was once one of the "Little Children Who Play the Horses."

Perhaps "Little Child" is an exaggerated phrase for the weedy youth just into his teens who arrived at the old United States Hotel in the early 1930s. Settled into a room next to my father, I quickly discovered what an adventurous place Saratoga was when I discovered a coil of rope next to the window with printed instructions above that opening indicating how I might, in case of fire, throw the unanchored end of the rope out the window and then lower myself by a wooden device entwined in the lifeline which regulated the speed of one's descent. In a safety-minded modern society which won't let so much as a gazebo be built without sprinklers and an alarm system, these Saratoga escape systems seem as primitive as the stone axe, and I speculated briefly as to how they would work for such heavyweight visitors to the hotel as Diamond Jim Brady and Jim Fiske.

Further sense of Saratoga's lively spirit came with my introduction to a fatherly pair of bookmakers, the Rogan brothers. In the '30s machines played no part in betting, which was on a credit basis with individual "Turf Accountants" of one's personal acquaintance.

The kindly Rogans gave me 2-1 on 8/5 shots and gave me a magic glimpse of a link with the colorful old days of mighty bettors, "Crazed," as Nellie Bly put it, "By the Mania for Gold." I was chatting with Mr. Jerry Rogan when a little old gentleman strolled by dressed as the "King of Dudes," Berry Wall, might have been for a day at the races. He had a white linen suit, pongee silk shirt with a high white stiff collar, black knit tie, straw boater, and the kind of bamboo cane which used to be called a "whangee."

Mr. Rogan informed me in an excited whisper that this was the famous John A. Drake, the man reputed to have bet a million dollars on a single race in England and to whom the risk of an occasional hundred thousand on a Saratoga afternoon had merely lent an extra savor to the afternoon's champagne.

I was informed that now, in his 90s, he occasionally bet a few hundred dollars "for laughs." As he passed on his way, lightly and gracefully swinging the bamboo stick through a nicely calculated arc, lifting his black-and-white-shod feet with no hint of a nonagenarian shuffle, I realized that he had not simply spent his life studying the mechanics of racing. He had given many hours to the arts of elegance, those arts which all good moralists denounce as trifling even as they secretly wish they had the hand of them.

One thinks of Queen Victoria denouncing her raffish and profligate uncles to Lord Palmerston only to hear that stylish old nobleman sigh, "But, Madam, they were such jolly men."

From Sir William Johnson on, visitors to Saratoga have come as pleasure seekers, Sir William and some subsequent pilgrims seeking to mend or extend their pleasures, and some, like Sophie Sparkles and her young friends, to catch bubbles before they burst. Some, like old Mr. Drake, were reduced to remembering bubbles, but like the Queen's uncles were still capable of laughter.

All of them came expecting the unexpected, the romance which made Saratoga Springs so different from the milltowns and agricultural centers which were its neighbors. If you happened to be spending the high season of 1839 at the Spa you could have seen Martin Van Buren, President of the United States, getting the cut direct at a formal ball from Mrs. De Witt Clinton, widow of his political rival.

If you were at the races on August 13, 1920, you would have seen the great Man O' War suffer his only career defeat when a bad start in the Sanford Stakes left him a neck behind the appropriately named Upset at the wire.

On other racing days you could have seen Jim Dandy at 100-1 defeat the great pair of Gallant Fox and Whichone in the Travers, or see Secretariat lose after a welcome in which every lamppost on Broadway was decorated with his blue and white colors.

If you chose the right moment to go to Cary Moon's famed Lake House restaurant you could have seen George Crum invent the potato chip. Whether it was done as a joke on a customer who complained about the thickness of his potatoes or as an inspired piece of cooking is now unknown. Historians who hold the view that the Saratoga chip was an inspiration rather than a demonstration of annoyance, ascribe the creation of the chip to Crum's colleague, "Aunt Katie" Weeks who, dropping a potato slice into some doughnut fat had sense enough not to throw it away after fishing it out and tasting it. The historians agree that the great moment, whether Crum's or Weeks', occurred in 1853, a year when the town was, in the words of a visitor, "First in manners, in dress, and in fashion to shine,/ Saratoga, the glory must ever be thine."

"Ever" is a stretch which outlasted even Petra, "the rose red city half as old as time," but Saratoga has been remarkable in that it has remained surprisingly proof against the vagaries of fashion, vagaries which have led Pied Piper'd throngs out of many resorts and spas over the years.

Even in the Depression Saratoga Springs flourished, although there were fewer Grand Dames competing for Mrs. De Witt Clinton's crown as Queen for the Season. The town's lifeblood in those years was supplied by the people whom Damon Runyon delighted to chronicle. Although gambling was theoretically illegal, roulette wheels spun steadily at such places as the Arrowhead Inn and the Chicago Club. The men and women to whom Runyon gave colorful names to cover their sometimes blood-colored occupations, swarmed into town to fill the places left empty by the parvenus whose pockets had been emptied by the crash.

If carriages no longer paraded on Broadway, the porches of Broadway's homes were filled by undershirted students of the Racing Form whose only complaint was that unfamiliar and distracting bird song kept them from concentrating on their figures.

The gentle humorist Frank Sullivan, a Saratoga native who died half a block from where he was born, wrote of the invaders, "They were a novelty, part of the seasonal fun, and most Saratogans rejoiced in their in-season guests, their high-spirited visitors, and were a little lonesome when they left." Giving directions to a visitor from New York, Sullivan once wrote, "As you get to the outskirts of Saratoga you'll spot the Spa and some white bathhouses on your left. A little farther on, off to the right, you will see a cemetery, placed there to remind the entering visitor that Saratoga is a health resort."

Of course, it was as a health resort that Saratoga Springs began, and still chiseled on the town's Hall of Springs are the words, "In this favored spot spring waters of life that heal the maladies of man and cheer his heart."

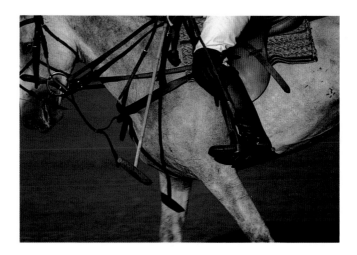

It is ironic that the place which began as a cleanser of the profligate should in time have encouraged so many of the excesses which the springs were supposed to ameliorate. Nothing can promise greater pleasure than the offering, however illusory, of health combined with happiness. The happiness might be achieved at the gaming tables, the dining tables, or the payoff windows of the racetrack—might also in later years be achieved through the sound of soaring strings or the sight of dancers afloat above the stage, while the health was to be achieved through a dip in those waters of life which the Iroquois guarded in the Kayadoroserra, "land of the crooked waters."

Many who were the Kings and Queens of Saratoga are forgotten and much that made it remarkable is gone. Potato chips are often made from mashed concentrate and Canfield is just the name of a game of solitaire, but the bright dawns that light up Saratoga Springs still remind one of the words of that old hedonist Logan Pearsall Smith who said, "When they can no longer sustain me with oysters and sips of champagne, I shall say with my last breath, you cannot be too fastidious."

Heywood Hale Broun

Spa Administrative Building

Queen of the Spas

Over 200 years ago on a battlefield near Saratoga Springs the tide of the American Revolution was turned, thanks to the heroic leadership of a colonial brigadier named Benedict Arnold. British General John Burgoyne surrendered on October 17, 1777. From that time to the present, the fortunes of Saratoga Springs have been as changeable as a gambler's luck.

Saratoga Springs was a favorite resort in the 19th century. Visitors flocked to this town in the foothills of the Adirondacks, about 185 miles north of New York City and twelve miles west of the Hudson River, for its mineral waters, mild climate, and lively society. In the early 1800s most people journeyed to "Putnam's Tavern & Boarding House" by stagecoach over rutted roads. Travel conditions improved in 1807 when it became possible to make the New York-to-Albany leg of the trip up the Hudson by steamer in less than 29 hours. The number of visitors further increased with the arrival of the first steam-propelled locomotive on July 3, 1833, three years after such passenger trains were introduced in the United States. By that time, Gideon Putnam had died, but his hotel, renamed Union Hall, was thriving. Before his death, Putnam landscaped his property adjacent to Congress Spring with flower-bordered paths, maples, and elms. Encouraged by the village board, the practice of planting flowers and shade trees became a custom in Saratoga Springs that continues to this day.

The springs which have attracted visitors to the area for years are each distinctive in taste and mineral content. Natural carbonation is said to make the mineral water more palatable than most. At the Baths, part of the spa ritual still includes a relaxing 20-minute session in a tub of the tiny bubbles, followed by a massage. In the 19th century, when visitors had more faith in the water's digestive benefits than they do today, "dipper boys" served therapeutic drafts in metal cups fastened to the ends of long sticks. At that time Congress Spring flowed at the rate of a gallon a minute, and by 1830, through the efforts of Dr. John Clark, 1,200 bottles of the sulfurous water were shipped each day throughout the nation and abroad; it was reputed to cure anything.

In the late 1800s the town's racetracks and casinos grew to be as well known as its mineral waters, and with these new pleasures came problems. In the early 1900s strong local and state antigambling sentiment closed the tracks and casinos. Few could afford to indulge in resort life during the Great Depression. During World War II gas rationing curtailed pleasure driving, and the racetrack was closed. In 1951, after the Kefauver Committee hearings, New York's Governor Dewey called for a special grand jury to investigate the role of organized crime in gambling; the casinos were closed, and Saratoga reached one of the lowest points in its history. Fortunately, the United States Urban Renewal Commission awarded a grant in the 1950s to revitalize the city. New highways improved transportation for both residents and tourists. Development of recreational facilities attracted more vacationers to the resort. Saratoga Springs now enjoys a prosperity unparalleled since the days when the town was the "Queen of the Spas."

The springs continue to flow, and some visitors continue to come to the Spa for "the cure," but the lavish hotels for which Saratoga was famous are gone. The Grand Union with its 306-foot dining hall, black walnut staircase, Waterford chandeliers, solid mahogany bar, and porch, said to be the world's longest at a quarter of a mile, was razed in 1953. The equally elegant United States Hotel is preserved solely in "Saratoga Trunk," the film version of Edna Ferber's novel. Only the old Adelphi Hotel, opened in 1877, stands today, its original interior completely restored as it was in an age not so unlike the present, when opulent pleasures were viewed with delight.

Big Red Spring, Saratoga Race Track

Row of buildings, built in 1871, Broadway

Clock, Adirondack Trust Company, Broadway

(Overleaf, pages 24-25) Spirit of Life, by Daniel C. French, Congress Park

(Overleaf, pages 26-27) Gideon Putnam Hotel, Saratoga Spa State Park

(Above and facing) Adelphi Hotel

Residential Saratoga

East of Saratoga Race Track in a wooded retreat, some of America's finest writers and composers gather to work. It is a place where artists are free from all but the demands of their own creativity. Carson McCullers called it "an emotional Shangri-la and literary Mecca." Its official name is Yaddo. Once the estate of the Spencer Trask family, it consists of 400 acres, a 55-room Victorian mansion, and a formal rose garden open to the public. According to legend, four-year-old Christina Trask's invention of a rhyming word for "shadow" gave Yaddo its name. After the deaths of their four young children, Spencer and Katrina Trask endowed the estate as a working retreat for artists. John Cheever described Yaddo as a place where "many men and women responsible for the vitality in American art have done their major work." Since opening in 1926, it has been a haven for over 2,300 guests including Eudora Welty, Saul Bellow, Katherine Anne Porter, Aaron Copland, Leonard Bernstein, Elizabeth Bishop, and William Carlos Williams. Sylvia Plath described the rooms as being like those in a castle. "The only sound is from the birds," she wrote, "and at night, the distant dreamlike calling of the announcer at the Saratoga racetrack."

From Yaddo, with its Tiffany windows, Tudor dining room, and Gothic embellishments, to the Queen Annes of Union Avenue and the Italianate villas of Broadway, Saratoga Springs' houses are as diverse as the people who have lived in them. Batcheller Mansion stands on Circular Street at the curve of Congress Park. Built between 1871-1873 for George Sherman Batcheller, U.S. representative to the International Tribunal in Egypt, the mansion fell into disrepair and was used for a time as a boardinghouse. Recent restoration shows Batchellor Mansion as its first owner knew it, a massive construction with sharply pitched gables, modeled on the chateaux of the Loire Valley.

Batcheller Mansion's imaginative designer may never have seen the French castles which inspired him. The architect-builders responsible for many of the town's magnificent houses usually relied on pattern books for the most fashionable styles of the day: Greek revival, Gothic revival, baroque, French chateau, Georgian, Italian villa, Queen Anne. Their adaptation of these popular plans to suit individual tastes injected a vigorous quality into already flamboyant if standard designs.

One of the handsomest residences along Broadway, a colonial revival built around 1906, was bought by Skidmore College in 1970 to serve as the President's house. With its Corinthian columns, Greek revival portico, Italianate brackets, and Queen Anne chimney, it incorporates in a single structure the variety which makes North Broadway a primer of 19th-century American architecture.

It was Skidmore's need for dormitory space that saved some of the mansions on Union Avenue from total deterioration during the Depression years, when the cost of maintaining such large private houses was prohibitive. Carriage houses were converted into classrooms, marble fireplaces were boarded up, and Skidmore girls moved into "singles" and "doubles" partitioned from the spacious rooms where Saratoga Springs' most socially prominent families once lived.

In the early 1970s, Skidmore, chartered as a woman's college in 1922, and now coeducational, moved to a new 1,200-acre campus. The houses of Union Avenue were sold. Some have been converted into apartments, and others restored to their former opulence. As in the past, owners of some "cottages" on North Broadway have estates elsewhere and come to Saratoga Springs only for the summer, although an increasing number are making this vital community their year-round home. A few permanent residents lease their houses during the summer, so that today, those not fortunate enough to own property in Saratoga Springs can live for a time in its special Victorian splendor.

(Pages 31-35) Yaddo

31

(*facing*) Spencer and Katrina Trask portraits

(Overleaf, pages 36-37) George S. Batcheller Mansion

Carriage house, Broadway

(*facing*) George S. Batcheller Mansion

President's home,
Skidmore College

(Pages 42-49) Private residences, Broadway

Social Events and the Arts

Henry James described Saratoga in 1870 as a place "where the greatest amount of dressing may be seen by the greatest number of people." It still is. Contemporary dandies may not be invited to a party like the one where Diamond Jim Brady is said to have worn 2,548 of his favorite stones, but the Saratoga season still offers ample opportunity to show off your wardrobe. The day might begin with breakfast at the track, then a round of golf or a few sets of tennis before a prerace luncheon. After the races, don a hat and white gloves for an afternoon of coaching, or black tie for an evening of dining and nostalgia in one of Saratoga Springs' historic landmarks. Tomorrow you might decide to enter a dog show disguised as your Dalmatian or spend the morning wrapped in hot sheets at the Spa. In any event, during August when Saratoga Springs' population swells to twice its usual size and a year's worth of social events is squeezed into a single month, dressing the part is just part of the fun.

The Whitney Ball opens the season. The ball's theme varies from year to year, but the setting remains the same, Canfield Casino in Congress Park. Built in 1870 by John Morrissey of Troy, the renowned gambling house was later bought by Richard Canfield. Canfield added paneled mirrors, gleaming chandeliers, and elaborate landscaping in keeping with the extravagance of his time, when as many as two million dollars were gambled in Saratoga Springs every weekday. The Casino, now on the National Register of Historic Places, houses the Historical Society of Saratoga Springs Museum, featuring exhibits on the town and its famous residents.

Guests at the National Museum of Racing's annual ball also enjoy an evening of music and dance in an atmosphere rich with history. The Museum and Thoroughbred Hall of Fame, which opened in 1955 after five years of temporary residency at Canfield Casino, display over 200 sets of racing silks, including those of the Queen of England and Sir Winston Churchill. There is a gallery of paintings by the great 19th-century equine artist, Edward Troye, and also such horse-racing memorabilia as a shoe worn by Kentucky, the first horse to win the Travers, and the boots and saddle used by jockey Johnny Loftus when he rode Man O' War.

Reflecting the community's ongoing concern for history, horses, and health, a number of Saratoga Springs' social occasions are not merely for fun. These activities benefit a variety of causes ranging from the National Museum of Dance, to equine research at Cornell, to therapeutic horseback riding. Entering the "Fattest Dog" competition will contribute to the Thoroughbred Retirement Fund, and dining at Riley's Lake House, an art deco casino restored for the special occasion, will aid in the fight against multiple sclerosis.

Saratoga Springs' cultural calendar is as full and varied as its social one, extending beyond the August season. The Saratoga Performing Arts Center, thanks to the inspiration and efforts of Robert McKelvey and the late Newman Wait, Jr., opened in 1966. Located in a natural amphitheatre in the 2,200-acre Saratoga Spa State Park, the Arts Center seats 5,100; there is room on the sloping lawns for 20,000 more. The open-sided pavilion has perfect acoustics and a specially constructed stage floor of southern yellow pine and tidewater cypress that make it well suited to both ballet and symphonic orchestra. It hosts the New York City Ballet in July and the Philadelphia Orchestra in August, and also attracts a wide range of other performers throughout the year.

Further enriching the area's cultural life is the National Museum of Dance, scheduled to open in 1986. Housed in the old Washington Bathhouse, the museum will allow visitors a unique opportunity to learn about the history of American professional dance and to observe young dancers improving their technique. Saratoga Springs, long associated with horses and high society, is increasingly a place where the arts share center stage.

Prerace luncheon party

Carriage ride to the Whitney Ball

Annual dog show

(Above and facing) Whitney Ball, Canfield Casino

54

(Above and facing) Annual ball, National Museum of Racing

Thoroughbred Hall of Fame, National Museum of Racing

Saratoga Golf and Polo Club

Private party, Riley's Lake House

(Pages 62-65) Saratoga Performing Arts Center

New York City Ballet performing with the Philadelphia Orchestra

Sales Ring and Backstretch

A gamble that may end at the finish line often begins at the Fasig-Tipton Yearling Sale, part of the Saratoga scene since 1913. During the second week of August, buyers from all over the world fill the Finney Pavilion, hoping to spot the new Man O' War. Built in 1968 and named for Humphrey Finney under whose management Fasig-Tipton attained international prominence, the Finney Pavilion is a place where buyers take risks that can reap large rewards. Dressed in black tie, company president John Finney presides over the annual event where bids that reach millions are given so discreetly only bid-spotters can note them.

Fasig-Tipton is a selected sale; roughly a fifth of the horses whose pedigrees are submitted to the company are chosen for auction. Five Kentucky Derby winners have passed through Fasig-Tipton's ring; the buyer at the Finney Pavilion is getting one of the finest yearlings in the country. Although the exceptional horse may earn up to four million dollars during his racing career and be syndicated for as much as six million dollars on retirement, most yearlings are not the exception. All must be trained, boarded, vetted, shod, and given time to grow. Keeping a racehorse at the track can cost up to $25,000 a year regardless of his earnings. For buyers who spend a quarter of a million dollars on a yearling at Fasig-Tipton, the expenses have only begun.

As a yearling, a horse is unproven, its value judged largely by bloodlines. Prospective buyers consult the catalogue and visit the sales stables to examine the animal. Many are looking for perfect conformation; all are hoping for what some horsemen call "heart," that unpredictable quality that gives a horse the will to win. No matter how studied and knowledgeable the purchase, luck plays a considerable factor; an investor may spend a fortune on a horse that never leaves the starting gate.

For many racing fans the excitement of the track begins at the moment the starting gate opens. On the backstretch, the day begins long before post time, as early as four in the morning. The horses are fed, groomed, saddled, and on the track before dawn. If the horse will race that day, his workout is short, chiefly to guarantee soundness. If the horse will not race that day, his morning workout is longer and more rigorous, a series of gallops over distance to build up endurance, interspersed with "blowouts," or sprints, to test speed.

Owners often watch the morning workouts from the clubhouse porch where they gather with other racing enthusiasts for breakfast, conversation, and the chance to observe the competition amid the sounds of hoofbeats and loudspeakers. While they are drinking orange juice on the porch, stable hands are cleaning out stalls on the backstretch, which at Saratoga Springs is a grassy, shaded area as colorful and charming as the clubhouse. Following the morning workout, the horses are washed with warm soapy sponges, hosed down, and walked until they are cool. Then, they are blanketed, returned to their stalls, fed, and allowed to rest.

For the horse who will race that day, the atmosphere is less relaxed. He is watered at mid-morning and fed oats for energy, but the hay is removed from his stall well before post time so that the animal doesn't fill up on the bulky food. Many horses sense the coming race from this change of routine even before they are examined by the track vet, led to the paddock, and saddled. There, the jockeys receive last minute instructions from the trainers, mount, and proceed to the track. Anticipation builds at the starting gate, where riders and horses are packed tightly into narrow stalls, waiting. The horses are nervous; the jockeys are tense, and the starter watches for the moment when the animals are still enough for him to begin the race safely. Then, a bell rings, stalls fly open, and the jockeys shout as the horses break clear of the gate.

(Pages 67-74) Fasig-Tipton Saratoga Yearling Sale

Finney Pavilion

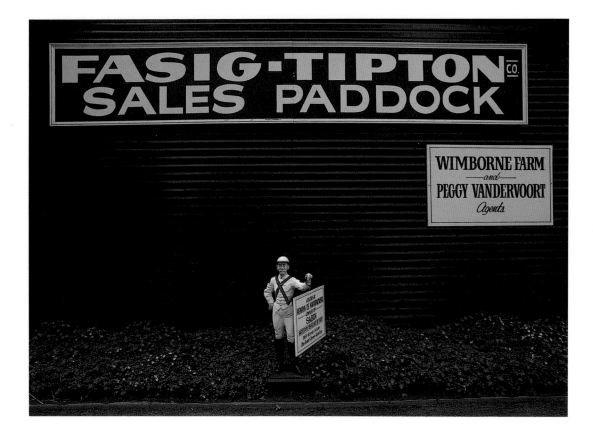

(Pages 75-79) Backside at the track

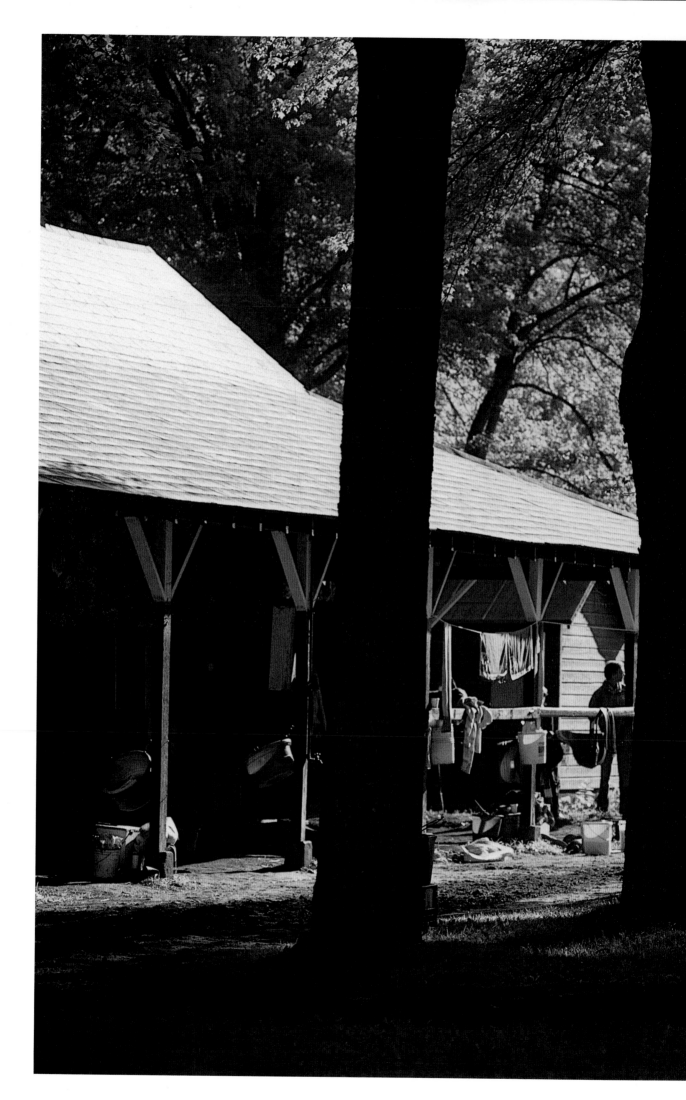

(Above and facing) Morning workout, Oklahoma Track

(Above and facing) Breakfast at the track

Horses and Sport

On August 3, 1864, a year after the first racing event confined to thoroughbreds was held in Saratoga Springs, the Saratoga Race Track opened through the efforts of John Hunter, William Travers, and Leonard Jerome (later to become Winston Churchill's grandfather). Two upsets highlighted the four-day event: the steeplechase when the favored Zig Zag lost his lead in a fall at the last hurdle, and the stake race when Hunter and Travers' horse Kentucky defeated Tipperary. Today, as in 1864, steeplechasing adds an element of variety to the racing program at Saratoga Springs, and the Travers, one of America's oldest stake races, is still being run and won by some of the best three-year-olds in the country. The Saratoga Race Track continues to attract thousands of people, rain or shine, for the 24 racing days of August.

Saratoga Race Track opened at a time when the Union Army's need for horses in Georgia must have seemed more important to some observers than the gamblers' need for horses at the races; pleasure has always been a priority at Saratoga. From the beginning the developers of the racetrack have devoted as much energy to creating elegant surroundings as to providing outstanding sport. The original covered viewing stand was equipped with clubroom and salons for its visitors' convenience and comfort. In 1865, the year the track was fenced, the grandstand seats were cushioned. In the early 1900s, when William Whitney (after whom the Whitney Stakes was named) was president of the Saratoga Racing Association, he introduced such new stakes as the Hopeful, and lengthened the track from a mile to a mile and an eighth, but he also remodeled the grandstand and added ornamental iron railings and gates.

Numerous improvements to the racecourse's sporting facilities have been made throughout its history, but rarely at the expense of its pastoral ambiance. Pennants grace the steeplechase hurdles. Flowers bloom by the porches. A canoe painted each year with the stable colors of the most recent Travers winner drifts among the ducks on the infield lake. Such decorative touches have helped to make Saratoga Race Track, one of the finest racecourses in the country, one of the most beautiful as well.

In the early 1900s, thoroughbred races were held at noon so that fans could attend the afternoon polo games. Today, visitors to Saratoga Springs still need not choose between the sports. On "dark" Tuesday afternoons in August when the track is closed, as well as on several other evenings during the week, some of the best polo players in the world join less experienced riders for fast-paced competition.

In the 1850s when Stephen Foster wrote about betting his "money on the bob-tailed nag," a horse named Flora Temple, harness racing was more popular and familiar to the crowds than "running horse" racing. The sport, whose official history in Saratoga Springs dates back to 1847 when 5,000 spectators watched Lady Suffolk beat the trotter Moscow, was also considered more respectable. Despite Foster's lyric, harness racing was not strongly associated with gambling. Unlike a thoroughbred race, a trotting race could be advertised as an "exhibit" with the horses' speed only part of the show. Today, horses trot as much against the clock as each other. Harness races are held nightly at the Saratoga Harness Track from mid-April through mid-November; in winter there is weekend racing. Since its opening in 1941, more records have been set and broken at the Saratoga Harness Track, than at any other half-mile track in the country.

The Saratoga Harness Track is adjacent to the thoroughbred racetrack, but the two sports have separate appeals. Their fans may have no more in common than the species they wager on and their passion for racing. Despite their differences, trotters, thoroughbreds, and polo ponies inspire a similar competitive fervor. Most horselovers agree that diversity is part of what makes Saratoga Springs so exciting, especially during August when the quality of equine sport, like the elegance of the town itself, is unparalleled.

(Pages 85-95) Saratoga Race Track

Original Man O' War Travers Cup

(Overleaf, pages 96-99) Polo, Saratoga Polo Club

Harness Race, Saratoga Harness Track

(Overleaf, pages 102-103) Steeplechase, Saratoga Race Track